The earth is mostly

W9-CAZ-290

The Earth Is Mostly Ocean

By Allan Fowler

Consultants

Robert L. Hillerich, Professor Emeritus,
Bowling Green State University, Bowling Green, Ohio;
Consultant, Pinellas County Schools, Florida

Norbert Wu, Marine Naturalist and Photographer

Lynne Kepler, Educational Consultant

Fay Robinson, Child Development Specialist

CHILDRENS PRESS®
CHICAGO

Design by Herman Adler Design Group
Photo Research by Feldman & Associates, Inc.

Library of Congress Cataloging-in-Publication Data

Fowler, Allan.
    The earth is mostly ocean / by Allan Fowler ; consultants,
  Robert L. Hillerich . . . [et al.].
      p. cm. – (Rookie read-about science)
    ISBN 0-516-06038-4
    1. Ocean—Juvenile literature. [1. Ocean.] I. Title.
  II. Series.
GC21.5.F69   1995
551.46–dc20   95-5562
                                                      CIP
                                                       AC

On a map or a globe of
the Earth, the blue parts
are water. The other
colors are land.

You can see that there is a lot more blue than all the other colors put together.

That's because most of the
Earth is covered by water
— the oceans.

The Pacific Ocean is
the largest. The Atlantic
is next, and then the
Indian Ocean.

The Arctic Ocean
surrounds the North Pole.

Much of its surface water
is frozen into ice.

The word "sea" is
sometimes used instead
of "ocean." But "sea" may
also mean a certain part
of an ocean.

For example, the
Caribbean Sea is part
of the Atlantic Ocean.

If you've ever gone swimming at an ocean beach, maybe you noticed that the water tasted salty. All ocean water has salt in it.

Water in lakes and rivers is not salty. We call it fresh water.

At one place, the Mariana Trench, the ocean floor is almost seven miles below the surface.

You could put the highest mountain on Earth in the Mariana Trench — and it would be completely under water!

Mt. Everest
29,028 ft. high
(above sea level)

sea level

Mariana Trench
36,056 ft. deep
(below sea level)

Most of the ocean bottom, or floor, is about 2 1/4 to 3 1/2 miles deep, and flat.

But, like the surface of the Earth, it also has canyons and mountains, even volcanoes.

Regular changes in the
level of ocean water are
called tides. Here is a
beach at low tide . . .
and the same beach at

high tide. The water has risen and covers more of the sand. On most coasts, about 12 1/2 hours pass between one high tide and the next.

What causes tides? The moon and the sun. They actually pull the ocean waters toward them.

The moon's pull is stronger, because it's much closer to Earth than the sun is.

20

Life in the oceans takes
many forms. Some of
them seem very strange.
There are animals that
look more like plants . . .

animals that live in shells . . .

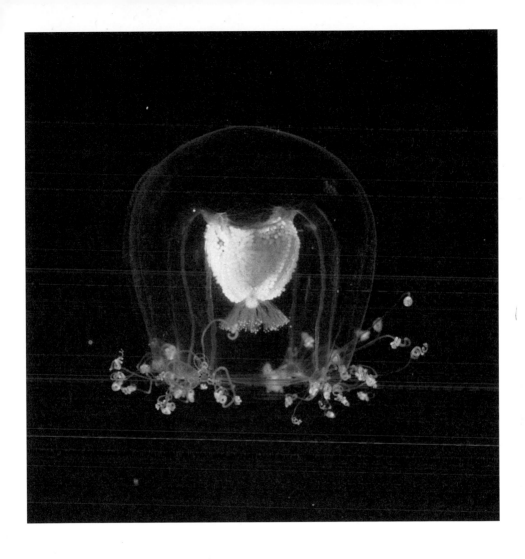

animals you can see through.

They share the ocean waters
with fish, thousands and
thousands of kinds . . .

and with marine mammals,
such as whales and dolphins.

Oceanographers are scientists who study the oceans. Some of them explore the depths in submersibles like this one.

Even where it's too deep for humans to go, submersibles are used — with no people on them. These probes have video cameras that send pictures to the ships above.

There is still much to be learned about the oceans.

It has been said that we know more about the surface of the moon than we do about the floor of our Earth's own oceans.

Words You Know

map

globe

ocean floor

low tide

high tide

submersible

ocean life

Index

About the Author

Allan Fowler is a free-lance writer with a background in advertising.
Born in New York, he lives in Chicago now and enjoys traveling.

Photo Credits